She the Confident

The Mindset Advantage
for Female Athletes

SHAY HADDOW

CONFIDENCE COACH FOR FEMALE ATHLETES

Table of Contents

Introduction

I developed a major confidence issue when I tore my ACL at the age of thirteen. Such insecurities never even crossed my mind before my injury. I was always one of the best players on my team. I could score, I was fast as lightning, and I could head the ball to Mars. However, after a long nine-month recovery, I was terrified to step on the field again—my teammates had been training and working hard while I was sidelined and could only watch.

If I thought that being injured was hard, I was in for a long road ahead. When I stepped back onto the field at almost fourteen years old, I wasn't as technically rusty as I thought I'd be. Of course, I was very out of shape and extremely timid, but even worse, my confidence was at an all-time low.

I had never experienced anything like that before. Instead of going out and playing the game I played my whole life, I second guessed every touch, decision, and movement I made. After all, how could I possibly keep up with my teammates that had been training for nine-months while I sat and watched?

Inner dialogue
dialogue
nibry dog

forever physical setback she overcomes, she brings up a mental block

After a lot of hard work, I got back into shape and cleaned up the rust that had accrued. While I lost nearly all of my speed, it seemed that I ~~also lost all~~ sense of self-belief and confidence as well.

I knew I could play the game without my speed, because I could outsmart the other team, but how could I possibly play to my full potential without the belief that I was good enough? This went on for two years.

I wasn't having fun in practice or games because I wasn't confident. I started to ride the bench way more often than I would have liked. When I was put into the game, I was so terrified of making a mistake that I played like a zombie. My only goal was to go out there and not make any mistakes. Guess what happened when I played like that? I sat on the bench even more, which truly made me doubt whether I was good enough to play and enjoy the sport I love.

I remember the exact moment when I almost cut the cord on my lifelong dreams…

It was September of my sophomore year. I was standing in the hallway, just about to walk out the door to drive to soccer practice for my club team. Before I walked out the door, I looked in the mirror that was on the hallway wall.

I looked miserable. I was miserable. I hated going to soccer practice. Soccer had become more of a chore than the game

I loved to play. The pressure I felt from my coaches and parents was starting to become too much for me to handle.

Even worse than the pressure, I felt that I wasn't good enough and didn't belong on my team. My other teammates were starting to talk to major Division I schools like North Carolina, Santa Clara, and BYU. Was I really good enough to play at a Division I school like the rest of my team? The clock was ticking, and I wasn't getting any hits from the big schools that I had emailed earlier that year. If I didn't go to a Division I school, I would be a failure... to myself, my family, and my teammates.

After taking a hard look into the mirror, I decided that it was all too much. I was going to talk to my dad about quitting so I didn't have to endure this feeling I felt anymore.

Now, I can't remember how that conversation went, but as you can guess, I decided to keep playing. We were only a few months away from the biggest tournament and recruiting opportunity of my career. If I could just go out and play with confidence and tenacity, then I had a shot at getting recruited.

I thank my lucky stars every day that I decided to stick it out. I went into that tournament with a mindset of leaving it all on the field. I knew that this was my chance to prove to myself that I was good enough and that I did belong.

We went on to win the tournament. More than that, I got my confidence back, played like the old me, and got recruited to play at a Division I school like I always dreamt about.

However, like any story, my soccer story didn't end there. All throughout my college career, I went through highs and lows in my confidence and self-belief. It wasn't until I finished my career that I developed the tools and strategies to build life-long confidence, and I can't wait to help you do the same.

Why I Wrote This Book

I know now that my struggles of confidence aren't unique to me. Ask any athlete, rock star, billionaire, or average Joe. We all struggle with confidence in our lives.

I know that as an athlete, and a female athlete specifically, that your confidence affects not only your performance but how you live your life. When I was going through my struggles as a teenager, I didn't have the resources or mentors to teach me how to be more confident. I just had to suck it up and deal with it.

I want more for you. I want to provide you with all the resources, tools, skills, and mentorship you need to be confident, happy, and successful in your sport, your academics, and your life.

I don't want you to go through what I went through. I don't want you to quit the sport you love because you believe that you aren't good enough. Because I promise, YOU ARE GOOD ENOUGH (and if I have to beat that into your head, I will).

Helping you overcome your self-doubt and develop life-long confidence is my life's mission. Whether you use it to become an all-star, a professional athlete, an artist, business person, or just an all-around bad ass, it is my goal to help you become the best YOU can possibly be. I can't wait to go on this journey with you.

Why It's Important You're Reading This Now

If you read this book, you will learn the skills and have the tools you need to be more confident and successful. Still, I want more for you.

In order to get the most out of this book and truly change your life, you must commit to the process. Commit to taking action after each chapter. Commit to practicing the skills you will learn. Just like any skill you want to master, becoming confident takes consistent practice.

I'll be honest, you won't magically become confident overnight, next weekend, or next month, but you'll start the process of doing so. It'll take time, patience, and hard work, but once you develop self-belief and confidence, there's no limit to what you can achieve in your sport or your life.

I know what you're probably thinking... "I don't have the time to work on being confident, I'm too busy with practice and school!"

Here's my answer to that: you will always be busy. It's never the "right" time to do the scary, uncomfortable thing. So, if you don't do it now, when will you do it?

Life is short, moves fast, and doesn't stop when you want it to. You are in control of your life and have the power to make the decision that NOW is the right time. Don't wait until tomorrow, Monday morning, or New Year's Day to take action.

Not only will this book help you to become a better athlete, student, and person, it will help you to transfer those skills into your life after sports. Whether you play a sport in high school or college, or even professionally, you will have a long life ahead of you after you're done playing your sport. Playing sports will teach you many of the life skills you need to be successful, and what you learn in this book will elevate your life even more. Read the book, take notes, practice these skills daily, and I promise, you'll see a shift in your confidence.

What to Do When
You're Done Reading This Book

Once you're done reading the entire book and taking action on each chapter, I want to help you on a deeper level!

Here are the steps to complete once finished:

Step 1: Visit my website at www.alphagirlconfidence.com to learn how I can personally help you in achieving lifelong confidence.

Step 2: From there you can book a free strategy session, we will go deeper into how I can help and go over full game plan to help you improve your confidence on and off the field.

Step 3 (for parents): Join us inside our free Facebook group for parents and coaches. In this group I host live trainings for parents every week that will help you to better support your daughter in becoming more confident on and off the playing field.

Request to join here:
www.facebook.com/groups/alphagirlconfidence

Part 1

Mindset

The Power of Mindset

> *"Mindsets are just beliefs. They're powerful beliefs, but they're just something in your mind, and you can change your mind."*
>
> – Carol Dweck

You've probably heard this word before, but what is a mindset? Let's put it into simple terms. Your mindset is made up of the beliefs you have about yourself, your abilities, and how you view the world around you. Ultimately, it's the foundation for how you live your life and what you accomplish or don't accomplish.

When you believe something, you will act in accordance to that belief. So, if you believe that you are a good student, you will act like a good student. If you believe that you are dumb, you will act dumb.

Essentially, what you believe affects your way of thinking, your attitude, and your behaviors. Your behaviors represent how you live your life. Let's break it down even more.

Let's say Molly believes that she can play professional soccer. If she believes this in her heart, she will see the world as full of opportunity if she puts in the effort. Her attitudes towards soccer, hard work, and becoming a professional athlete will align with her belief that she can make it. Her behaviors will include training hard, getting extra help from coaches, taking care of her nutrition, lifting weights, and whatever else she believes will help her get there. Having this mindset leads to all the behaviors that will allow her to be successful as a professional athlete.

Now let's take a look at another example on the opposite side of the spectrum.

Sarah believes that since her parents dropped out of high school, that she will too. If she believes that she will indeed fail and drop out of high school, then she will see the world as lacking opportunities and see herself as a victim. Her attitude towards school and academics will be poor. She won't do her homework, won't study for tests, and will be disruptive in class. By having this mindset, it leads to these behaviors which will confirm her belief that she will drop out of high school.

Here's the amazing thing about mindset, we have complete control over our mind and have the ability to change our mindset, which CAN CHANGE YOUR LIFE!

If you take a look at the examples above, each person had a different mindset. Molly has a mindset that allows her to see the world as a place of growth and abundance. Sarah has a mindset that shapes her destructive behaviors and see's the world as lacking.

We Call this Growth Mindset and Fixed Mindset

"Whether you think you can or can't, you're right."
                                    – Henry Ford

With a growth mindset, you believe that you can learn and grow with time and effort, that your abilities and intelligence can change and improve. People with a growth mindset take on new challenges, see failure as an opportunity to learn, are open to criticism and being taught, have a passion for hard work, and know that growing is a process. Ultimately, they believe that anything is possible with time and consistent effort. Having a growth mindset leads to endless growth and fulfillment.

With a fixed mindset, you believe that your abilities are fixed, that you can't get better at something, and that talent, not effort, is what creates success. People with a fixed mindset avoid challenges, resist criticism, and fear failure. This mindset is destructive and leads to pain and stagnation.

Which mindset do you want to have? Use the following table to honestly think about which one sounds more like you.

FIXED MINDSET	GROWTH MINDSET
I'm either good at it or I'm not.	I can learn and do anything I want.
I give up when it's too hard.	Failure is an opportunity for learning.
I stick to what I know.	I like to try new things.
I don't like to be challenged.	Challenges help me to grow.
I take feedback and criticism personally.	I welcome feedback.

You may see a few from each side that sound like you, and that's okay! Luckily, we have complete control over our mind and have the ability to change from a fixed mindset to a growth mindset! You may have a growth mindset in some areas of your life, such as your sport, and you may have a fixed mindset in other areas, such as learning how to play an instrument. The goal is to develop a growth mindset with every area of your life, and you'll learn just how to do that in the next chapter!

Changing Your Mindset

> *"Once your mindset changes, every-thing on the outside will change along with it."*
>
> *– Steve Maraboli*

Changing your mindset isn't as simple as changing your outfit (bummer, I know). However, once you break through and change your mindset, it's like the heavens open above you and you'll see the world, your life, and yourself, in a whole new light. So yes, it takes time and practice to change your mindset, but the good thing is that nothing can stop you from changing your mindset, except for you.

Buckle up, because before finding true fulfillment and success in life, you MUST develop a growth mindset, and here are the strategies to shift you from a fixed to a growth mindset.

Try Something New

We are all capable of trying and learning a new skill, whether it's small like how to make a paper airplane or big like how to fly an airplane. By trying something new, you will prove to yourself that you can learn something new and get better at it. The more you try new things and learn the skills to be good at it, the more you will start to believe that you can learn and do anything you desire with time and effort, which will start to shift you into a growth mindset.

An example of something simple you can do is to practice writing with your non-dominant hand. Spend five minutes writing every day for a few days. I'm betting the quality of your writing will improve every single day, even after just a few minutes of practicing.

Use Past Experiences - Look for Evidence

We all have past experiences where we did something that we didn't know how, and then did it! You learned how to walk, talk, write, tie your shoes, ride a bike, etc. You've learned how to improve at something and learn something new in the past. And guess what? You can do it again!

If you're feeling like you're stuck and can't get better or learn a new skill, do the following:

- STOP and take a deep breath.
- Consider three things that you originally didn't think you could do that you eventually learned how to do (can be big or small).
- Go do that thing you're trying to get better at with a new mindset that you can do it.

Celebrate Small Wins

I keep a daily planner, and every night before I go to bed, I write down my three wins for the day. I do this no matter how big or small these were. For you, this could be scoring a goal in your scrimmage, getting a tutor for math class, or having a healthy dinner. The point here is that it doesn't need to be earth shattering to be a win.

When you take the time to write down your wins, it does a few things:

First, it helps you to focus on the positive throughout your day. For most of us, we have a much easier time remembering the bad than the good. If you had a tough day, I bet that you only think about the bad stuff, and that quickly leads to thinking that the day was all bad. In reality, you just had bad moments, and those bad moments overtake anything good that happened. So yes, you may have what you think is a bad day, but if you step back and think about the big picture, I promise you can find small wins in the worst of days. By writing down the good, you are training your mind to find the good in your day.

Second, you are proving to yourself that you are capable of doing awesome things. When you do this on a consistent basis, it serves as a journal to lift you up when you're down. When you feel like you suck at everything, all you have to do is open up your journal and look at all your past wins to re-affirm that you are successful, good enough, and have the power to do awesome things.

Embrace and Learn from Failure

I know what you're thinking: "But I hate failing! Failing makes me think I'm not good enough." Trust me, I hate failing just as much as the next person.

Here's the thing about failure: it's not the end! It's actually quite the opposite. Although failure makes you feel like crap and may close one door, it opens up possibility for new opportunities and growth.

There are hundreds of wildly successful people in this world that have failed miserably but ended up bouncing back and being the G.O.A.T. ("greatest of all time"). Here are a few stories to prove it to you!

MICHAEL JORDAN

In 1978, sophomore Michael Jordan tried out for the varsity basketball team at Laney High School. When the list was posted, Jordan's name wasn't on it. Instead, he was asked to play on the junior varsity team after expecting and working to make the varsity team.

After picking himself up off the floor, Jordan did what champions do. He let his failure and disappointment drive him to be better. He played on the junior varsity team, and he worked himself to the limit.

He then went on to play at North Carolina and became a star college player. Then he played for the Chicago Bulls, won six NBA titles, five MVP titles, and is considered by most to be the best to ever step on the court.

JK ROWLING

Rowling is one of the most inspirational success stories of our time. You probably know her as the author who created *Harry Potter.* What most people don't know is what she went through prior to being hugely successful.

When Rowling wrote the first Harry Potter book, she was divorced, bankrupt, on welfare, and a single mother. After several publishers rejected her manuscript, one finally agreed to publish it. At the same time, the publisher told Rowling that she needed to get a job because there's no money in children's books. Rowling is now a billionaire and has sold over 500 million copies of the *Harry Potter* books.

> *"You might never fail on the scale I did, but it is impossible to live without failing at something, unless you live so cautiously that you might as well not have lived at all—in which case, you fail by default."*
>
> *– JK Rowling*

So, next time you fail a test, get cut from a team, or miss that shot, just think of the stories above and realize that failure is a part of life. It's about dusting yourself off, looking at the opportunities for growth and learning, and going out to take on the next challenge!

Action steps to complete:

1. Identify if you currently have a fixed or growth mindset

2. If you have a fixed mindset, identify what's causing that fixed mindset

3. Start a daily journal: write three daily wins before you go to bed

Progress, Not Perfection

"Perfection is the enemy of progress."

– Winston Churchill

Having the mindset of always being perfect will rob you of progress, happiness, and success. Perfection and the fear of failure is what stops so many people from doing what they love and living their dreams.

I see this every day when I coach players who aren't willing to try something new because they know they won't get it perfect, players who slump their shoulders and give up when they don't complete the perfect pass. Because of this need to always be perfect, they aren't willing to push themselves out of their comfort zone or improve upon their weaknesses.

To get away from this need to be perfect, there's a simple phrase you can use to drastically shift your mindset. I learned this phrase from one of my mentors, Marie Forleo, and that is…

"Progress, not perfection."

Look, I know what you're thinking… "But Coach Shay, I take pride in my work and want it to be the very best it can possibly be!"

Yes, it's important to hold yourself to high standards, but perfectionism and high standards are not the same thing. Holding yourself to high standards is healthy and motivates you to perform your best. Perfectionism is rooted in fear of failure, looking bad, making a mistake, being judged. It all comes down to this one main fear: that you aren't good enough.

Instead of striving to be perfect, strive for progress! When you strive for progress, you take consistent action to get things done. When you only strive for perfection, you will stop as soon as it gets hard or failure is near. Perfection will stop you from trying something challenging and getting out of your comfort zone.

Next time you work on a project or learning a new skill, think progress over perfection. **Getting something done imperfectly is better than not doing anything at all!** Here's proof that progress is always better than perfection.

In May of 2018 I held my first paid soccer clinic. I had just had a free clinic the month prior and had over 20 girls there. So I was sure that my paid clinics would be just as much of a hit, right?!

WRONG!

My clinics were open to twelve girls at the time, and guess how many showed up... three. I was so embarrassed that I couldn't get more girls to come. I had a clinic scheduled for every month that year going forward, and I was terrified that they would all turn out like this. I had a million thoughts of self-doubt running through my head.

"Was I a bad coach?"
"Was I charging too much?"
"Can I really do this?"

Now, I could have easily refunded the money of the three girls that showed up and called it a day because of the embarrassment I felt. But I did the clinic anyway and with a great attitude. I wanted to give those girls the best hour of training that I could.

Going into the next month was the Spring Break Clinic, a two-day event focused on attacking and defending. I even got shirts for any of the girls that signed up, so I was sure that I was going to fill it up this time. Free shirts and Spring Break, who could say no?

This time, seven girls signed up. Sure, I could have been disappointed again that it didn't fill up, but it was *progress!* I knew that this was going to take time to develop and would take time to make more connections and reach more girls. That year, I had two clinics sell out and no fewer than eight girls signed up.

At the end of 2018, I wanted to challenge myself. I believed that if I could get twelve girls signed up, that I could get eighteen. So, in 2019, I opened up my first clinic to eighteen girls, and guess how many signed up? You got it, all eight-een! The following clinics after that have since sold out, and some within three days! Heck, I even had to hire another coach to help me because the clinic had too many girls!

If I wouldn't have used the progress not perfection mindset, I would have never grown to where I am today. It would have been a lot easier to stop doing clinics because I feared failure and embarrassment of what other people thought.

Progress is never straightforward. There will be times when you make progress, and then you end up right where you started. However, when you strive for progress, not perfection, I promise that you will, over time, see huge leaps from where you started. With that mindset, it will allow you to push through the hard times and never give up on what matters to you.

Action steps to complete:

1. Think back to one or two times where you failed (write it down)
2. How did that failure help progress you to get better? What did you learn from it?
3. Repeat this every time you fail going forward

1. a) failing a squat weight after vacation that i had previously moved easily

b) i got a 59 on my calc test, never happened before, new exp.

2. worked harder when feeling weak rather than just pushing when strong, saw teacher every week, understanding

Part 2
Confidence

The Ultimate Super Power

> *"As far as self-confidence goes, so much of social media is about approval, getting likes, comparing our lives to others' - meanwhile, confidence is an inside job: it's about how you feel about yourself regardless of what anyone else does or thinks. It's a knowing that you're human, you're flawed, and you're awesome in your own way."*
>
> – Jen Sincero

As I already mentioned at the beginning of the book, I struggled with confidence throughout my whole playing career—from the youth level and all the way through my college career. I thought I had it figured out when I finally got recruited and committed to play at a Division I school, but nope, I was about to go on another confidence roller-coaster ride!

When I first got to VCU, although extremely terrified, I had prepared well over the summer. I passed all of the fitness and technical tests that were required of us during preseason camp. But as soon as I stepped on the field and had to compete... *sheeesh!* I felt like a little troll amongst giants! Not that I was physically smaller than them, but I felt in my play that I was so small. They played so fast and so aggressively, I felt like I was drowning trying to keep up.

During that freshman season, it took me some time to get the hang of things. I didn't play much at first, but eventually I started to gain more confidence and even ended up starting a few times and getting some good minutes in.

Fast forward to my transfer to Utah State. Even though that was my home state, and I had old friends on the team, I was terrified. I felt like an outsider who was intruding on this team mid-year. All the girls had already formed relationships and bonds with each other, and I had to play catch up. Contrary to the fall semester of my freshman year, I was NOT in shape coming into Utah State. I started during the spring semester, which is pretty much equal to Hell: 6:00am weights and 7:00am conditioning (when it's 15 degrees) is not fun, trust me!

As you can imagine, I was not confident in the least bit that semester. Heading into my sophomore fall season, I learned from my mistake of not being in shape, and felt like I had something to prove during pre-season camp. I worked my butt off that summer in order to feel more confident and gain the respect of my coaches and teammates. My sophomore season was finally the year that I started to gain traction and some real confidence on the field. I had an awesome upperclassmen that took me under her wing and showed me how the position should be played.

Going into my junior season, I knew I was going to be one of the top few players on the depth chart for my position. However, just a few days into pre-season, I went down with a knee injury in practice: torn Meniscus (again). Luckily it was a super easy surgery and I was able to walk out of there on my own power, so the recovery would only be about six weeks.

Well, in that six weeks, I lost my spot. That's the sucky thing about getting injured... your spot is never guaranteed. Trying to get my spot back that season was the toughest year of my whole college career. I got less playing time than I had the previous year, and it was obvious that I was unhappy. I wasn't being a good teammate while I was on the bench and when I was on the field, I was terrified of making mistakes because I didn't want to get pulled out. It was obvious that my head wasn't in the right place. I never got my spot back that season, even though we ended up winning the conference tournament and going to the NCAAs for the second time in a row.

Going to the NCAAs is an amazing feat. Only 64 teams in the whole country get to do so, yet, I wasn't happy, I wasn't confident, and I wasn't playing. Thinking back on it, my lack of confidence blocked any sense of accomplishment or joy because I was so focused on what was going wrong.

Fast forward to my Senior year. While my knee was giving my trouble in the beginning of pre-season camp, I was committed to taking responsibility for my own playing time and my own confidence. Again, I worked my butt of in order to be prepared to get my spot back. I was voted team captain, which lit a huge fire under my butt to be the best player and teammate I could that year. I got my spot back and had the best season and some of the best games of my life. I was more confident and focused than ever before, and most importantly, it was the most fun I ever had playing soccer.

So, what role did confidence play in my career? To me, it was EVERYTHING. Having confidence helped me perform better, be a better leader, work harder, and ultimately have more fun doing what I loved. Going through my confidence roller-coaster and coming out on top, helped me to be more confident in every area of my life, and gave me the tools I needed to help others do the same. In the coming chapters, I will teach you actionable strategies to improve your confidence that you can use in your daily life, on and off the field.

Strategy #1: Practice and Preparation

"Practice creates confidence. Confidence empowers you."

– Simone Biles

The first and most obvious strategy to improve your confidence is to practice and prepare!

If you want to get better at something, you need to practice! If you want to learn how to play the guitar, you'll take lessons or watch videos on YouTube, and you'll practice what you learned to become better and more confident.

Same goes for taking a test. If you have a big test coming up and don't prepare for it, you'll most likely feel terrified to take it and get cold sweats because you didn't take the time to prepare.

You go to practice every week to get better at your sport, right? The more competent you are at a certain skill, the more confident you'll be performing that skill.

If you've got an awesome right-footed shot, you'll be confident in your ability to shoot with you right foot. Conversely, if you aren't as good with your left foot, you won't be confident when using it and you'll probably avoid it at all costs.

One of the worst things you can do if you aren't good at something that you want/need to improve on is avoid practicing it! I get it. It's much more fun to practice something you're good at. Practicing your weaknesses is embarrassing cause you might look awkward or mess up, but if you truly want to become better and more confident, you have to practice!

When it comes down to it, you have two options:

Option 1: Only focus on practicing your strengths and get really good and really confident doing it while avoiding practicing your weaknesses. You'll be much more comfortable this way and won't risk embarrassment, but your weakness will always stay that way and you'll never be fully confident in your ability.

Or

Option 2: Focus on practicing your weaknesses so that you can become better and more confident over time. You'll risk looking dumb, feeling awkward, and failing, but with effort, patience, and time, you'll become just as confident and be able to turn it into one of your strengths. You can repeat this same thing for any new skill you want to learn or get better at.

Which one will you choose? The easy route (option 1) or the more difficult but rewarding route (option 2)? If you choose option 2, there's nothing that can stop you, except

YOU! Realize that it will take consistent action, hard work, and patience to see improvements. But you can do it!

Next time you want to get better and improve your confidence, I hope you'll take option to in order to become more confident in that skill and in your overall ability to improve at anything.

Action steps to complete:

1. Write down the top two things you want to improve on.
2. Next to each thing, write down what you need to practice in order to get better. Be specific here!
3. Schedule it into your calendar.

- blocking work
- moving lateally in defense

1. foot work, over passes, core engagment, piking, shoulders
2. shuffles, mindset, run throughs

Strategy #2: Controlling Your Inner Voice

"Change your thoughts and you change your world."

– Norman Vincent Peale

We all have an inner voice. Sometimes it's helpful, and sometimes it can be destructive. You hear your own voice far more than you hear anyone else's voice, and it is by far the most powerful voice you will ever hear! The constant chatter in your mind (your inner voice) will shape your beliefs, which lead to actions or behaviors, which will ultimately dictate how you live your life.

Thoughts → Beliefs → Actions

Whether your inner dialogue is good or bad, the things you continually say to yourself will shape your beliefs about yourself and your abilities and what you believe will come to be. If you tell yourself your whole life that you're horrible at math, you will be horrible at math. On the flip side, if you tell yourself that you will become a pro athlete, chances are that you will become a pro athlete. Remember, your beliefs lead to your actions.

When you believe that you're bad at math, your actions will line up with that. You won't take the time to learn, study, or improve because in your mind, you're just bad at it and cannot improve regardless of the effort. If you believe that you will be a pro athlete, you'll take the necessary actions to make it happen.

Your mind has the power to do amazing things, and luckily, you have total control over your mind and inner voice. You have the power to change your thoughts, your beliefs, and your actions in order to change your life.

By simply changing your destructive thoughts into positive ones, your mindset will shift into that of a growth mindset. Your belief and confidence in yourself will be elevated. Of course, changing your inner voice isn't always easy. It is all too common that negative thoughts repeat to the point of becoming bad habits that we continue to develop over our whole lives. Changing from negative thoughts to positive thoughts is simple, but it takes practice and awareness of your current thoughts and effort to change those thoughts into helpful ones.

So, the first step to changing your inner voice is to observe your thoughts. Pay attention to how you talk to yourself. Take note of when you have negative thoughts and when you have positive ones.

Once you are more aware of your own thoughts, you can start to change them. Instead of just having the thought and moving on, next time you have a negative thought, you must STOP and change that negative thought into a positive one.

Here are some common examples of negative thoughts that can be changed to positive ones

Example 1:
Negative thought: "I'm too slow and will never be able to stop their forward."

STOP and reassess that thought.

Positive thought: "I may not be as fast as her, but I'm smarter and can use angles to cut her off and keep her in front of me."

Example 2:
Negative thought: "I'm not skilled enough to make the varsity team."

STOP and reassess that thought.

Positive thought: "By being the hardest working player on the field, I can improve my skills and show the coaches how valuable I can be to the team."

Example 3:
Negative thought: "I'm too dumb to learn how to speak Spanish."

STOP and reassess that thought.

Positive thought: "I can learn anything I want with time, effort, and a good teacher."

Remember, the first step to changing your inner voice is to be aware of the negative thoughts that enter your mind. Every time you have a destructive thought about why you can't do something or that you aren't good enough, you must first realize that the thought is happening and that it needs to be changed. From there, you can flip the negative into a positive.

Using Affirmations to Improve Confidence

Using affirmations is one of the best ways to change your inner voice and ultimately help you to feel more confident. Affirmations are positive statements that can help you challenge and overcome self-sabotaging and negative thoughts. When you repeat them often, and believe in them, you can start to make positive changes.

According to researchers, spending just a few minutes thinking about your positive qualities before a game or performance can help calm nerves, improve confidence, and increase your chances of success. Even more than just thinking about your affirmations, if you go a step further and SAY and WRITE your affirmations, it will give them more power.

How to Write Your Own Affirmations

1. Turn negative statements into positive statements. Just like you read earlier in changing your negative thoughts, the same thing will be used when writing down your affirmations.

2. Write your affirmation in the present tense as if it's already happening. For example, "I am prepared, confident, and will have a great game today," is a great affirmation if you're nervous before playing in a game.

3. Write it, say it, believe it! The more emotion you put into your affirmation, the more weight it will carry. You may not believe it the first time or even the first few times you say it, but with consistency, you will start to believe it as fact and that will change your life.

Here are some examples of affirmations to get you going:

- I am a good player
- I am fast
- I am a good student
- My team respects me
- I enjoy working with my team
- I will get a good grade on my test
- I have everything I need to be successful
- I am a good friend
- My hard work will pay off

Now it's your turn!

Action steps to complete:

1. Write down all of the negative thoughts and beliefs you have about yourself.

2. Next to each negative thought, write out a positive one to replace it that will help you grow.

3. Get a journal and write down one positive affirmation every day when you wake up.

- im not fast enough
  ↳ I am faster than I was at the beginning of summer
- I am too short
  ↳ my approach jump has improved
-

Strategy #3: Visualization

"Visualize what you want to do before you do it. Visualization is so powerful that when you know what you want, you will get it."

–Audrey Flack

Out of all of the strategies you will learn, visualization is my personal favorite. It's easy to do, it's free, and it only takes a few minutes. Before we get into how to use visualization, you must first understand what it is and why it works. Visualization is the process of creating a mental image or intention of what you want to happen or feel in reality. So essentially, it's like creating a movie in your mind of what you want to happen in real life.

There are many benefits of visualization before you play a sport, take a test, or perform in an event, here are a few:

- Boosts confidence
- Calms nerves and gets you in a relaxed state
- Prepares your body to perform how you intend it to
- Helps the brain recall facts, movements, and information

Visualization is an extremely simple, yet effective way to improve confidence and get prepared before a game. It can be done virtually anywhere and anytime. I suggest doing it either the night before your game before you go to sleep, on your way to the game (if you aren't driving), or as soon as you get to the field before warmups. Visualization can also be used to help calm your nerves and make you more confident before a test or presentation.

I recently had to give a speech at a city council meeting and was beyond terrified. I love speaking in front of youth and teenagers, but speaking in front of powerful people in my community was a lot less comfortable for me! The morning of the speech, I knew that if I could use the tools of preparation and visualization, not only would I be calmer, but I would crush it! After I prepared the speech and practiced it a few times, I sat down on my couch and closed my eyes. I settled into my breathing to slow my heart rate down. Then I went through every part of that speech, from arriving at the venue, walking up to the microphone, and performing the speech with confidence. I even visualized how amazing I would feel once I was done!

Guess how my speech went? You guessed it! Better than I could have ever imagined. Visualization is such a powerful tool to help you be confident and successful! Here's how to use it.

How to Visualize

One of the biggest reasons why visualization is so effective for athletes is because of how simple it is to do. Any athlete, ranging from five years old to 100 years old, can learn how to visualize effectively.

Here's how to get the most out of your visualization:

Step 1: Find a quiet space *without distractions* (feel free to use headphones).

Step 2: Close your eyes and get comfortable (seated or laying works here).

Step 3: Imagine yourself arriving to your game and seeing/feeling the following things:

How do you feel? Is it hot or cold outside? What are you wearing? Where are you playing? Who are you playing? What do you smell?

Step 4: Visualize yourself going through your warmups. How do you feel? How are you playing? Are you excited and ready to play?

Step 5: Imagine the starting whistle blowing and go through the game in your head. Imagine yourself making awesome plays on both sides of the ball. Imagine the celebration when you score or get an assist. Visualize yourself crushing your weaknesses or things that you don't feel confident about. The more detailed you can get, the better. Spend the majority of your time on this step.

Here are some position specific examples for soccer players to go through:

- **Forward:** imagine yourself making a run to receive the ball, dribbling and cutting past a defender, and then taking an awesome shot, finishing with a goal.

- **Midfielder:** visualize yourself winning a header out of the air, and then getting a wall pass from your teammate, playing the ball up to a forward, and getting an assist.

- **Defender:** visualize yourself jockeying for position against an attacker, winning the ball in a solid tackle, and distributing the ball to keep possession.

- **Goalkeeper:** imagine that an attacker has a wide-open shot on you but you're ready for it. As the attacker winds up to take the shot you read her eyes and can see which direction her shot is going, and you make an amazing diving save.

Step 6: Open your eyes and go do what you just visualized!

As you can see, by imagining yourself being successful in your mind, you will have a huge boost in confidence and overall feelings of excitement to get on the field and perform what you just imagined.

Don't get discouraged if you have a hard time focusing and visualizing in great detail the first few times. Like any skill, visualization must be practiced. Sitting still and just being is much harder than you'd think, especially in today's world. The first few times you attempt it, you'll probably feel like you should be doing something else with your time. You may get bored and rush through it because sitting still and visualizing can be uncomfortable, but it's important to follow through with it anyways! The more you do it, the easier it will come and the more effective it'll be, so stick with it and stay patient.

If you visualize for the first time and don't have a stand-out game, that's okay! It may not work the first time or every time you do it. By staying consistent and doing it before every game, you'll develop your visualization muscle and you'll start to see progress each and every time you do it.

Using Visualization While Injured

Unfortunately, like in my story, suffering from an injury can be a huge hit to your confidence. The stress of losing your spot, getting out of shape, and losing your skill takes a toll on your mental well-being and confidence levels. Luckily, visualization is an amazing tool that can be used for injured players to help them stay motivated and sharp mentally. Using visualization as an injured player can help an athlete cope with the emotional effects of being injured and stay positive throughout the rehabilitation process. Visualizing past performances helps the athlete retain motor skills that they may otherwise lose if injured for long periods of time.

Stepping back onto the field or court after an injury can be scary to say the least. Thoughts of self-doubt may start to creep in about whether or not you're really ready to come back, if you'll get injured again, or if you will be as good as you were before your injury. When those thoughts start to creep in, visualization can be your best friend.

As you're nearing the end of your rehab and getting ready to step back onto the field, using visualization will help to erase those negative thoughts and get your mind and body into a confident state where you're ready and excited to compete!

Action steps to complete:

1. Practice visualization for five minutes before your next game/event.
   a.) Be detailed: where are you, how do you feel, what's the
      weather like?
   b.) Visualize specific plays you want to make.

2. Pay attention to how you feel after you do it.

3. Build a habit to spend five minutes visualizing before every game.

4. If injured, add ten minutes of weekly visualization to your rehab process.

Strategy #4: Body Language

> *"Smile even if you don't feel like it. Your body language helps determine your state of mind."*
> – Gitte Falkenberg

Imagine you're lined up across the field from a team before the kickoff. Most of the players are standing tall and look like they're ready to roll, but there's one player standing right across from you who is looking down, her shoulders are slumped, and she's fidgeting with her jersey. You take one look at her and can smell the lack of confidence oozing out of her. You have never talked to her or even seen her until now. So how is it that you know she's not confident?

Body language!

People read your body language, often without even thinking. Our posture and poses reflect our mood and our confidence levels. We stand and walk a certain way when we're confident and another way when we're nervous.

The more confident you are, the more you'll stand tall, hold your shoulders back, and make eye contact. Conversely, when you're not confident, you'll slump your shoulders, hold your head down, and find something to fidget with. Here's the crazy thing: we can trick our minds into thinking we're confident just by changing our body language. If you're nervous and lack confidence, try to hold poses of confidence. You'll start to notice a change in how you feel.

Refer to the table below to learn the difference between confident body language and non-confident body language.

POSITIVE BODY LANGUAGE	POOR BODY LANGUAGE
Eye contact	Avoids eye-contact
Shoulders back (good posture)	Slumped shoulders
Head held high	Head down
Wide stance	Narrow stance
Smile	Frowning or fake smile
Relaxed arms	Fidgeting with pockets, clothes, hair

So, next time you're not feeling confident, adjust your body to match that of a confident person. You'll see your mindset start to shift to help you become more confident.

In addition to using body language to become more confident, body language will also play a role in how your coaches and teachers perceive your attitude and effort.

If your goal is to get recruited to play your sport in college, scouts will pay very close attention to your body language. How you hold yourself during warmups, when you get scored on, and when you're up a goal will all play a big role in how attractive you are to that scout. If you have poor body language, the coach will see that and think that you're lazy or have a bad attitude. They will pay very close attention to how you hold your body when you make a mistake or how you react after a loss.

When I go watch games, I can always tell which player really cares and wants to be there and which player is just going through the motions, all based on their body language. If you're unaware of what your body language looks like while you're playing, then have your parents record you even if it's just for a few minutes.

Body language, as insignificant as it seems, plays a huge role in every area of your life. Pay attention to how you hold yourself now because when you're done playing your sport, it will determine whether or not you get the job, the promotion, or the recognition you deserve.

Action steps to complete:

1. Pay attention to how you hold your body in times of nervousness or anxiousness.

2. Change poor body language to positive body language.

3. Record yourself during games to get a better idea of how to improve your body language.

Strategy #5: Surround Yourself with Positivity

"Surround yourself with good people; surround yourself with positivity and people who are going to challenge you to make you better."

– Ali Krieger

One of the hardest but most important decisions to make is to surround yourself with positive people. The people you surround yourself with will either help or hurt your confidence and growth. I know you can't choose your parents, siblings, or coaches, but you do have control over the friends you decide to surround yourself with.

You are the average of the five people you spend the most time with. So, if you hang out with people that are negative, lazy, Debbie downers, then you will become just like them. On the other hand, if you surround yourself with people that are positive, hardworking, confident, and ambitious, then you will level-up to be on the same wavelength as them.

When it comes down to it, a lot of humans are like crabs. If you were to put a bunch of crabs into a large bucket here's what would happen: a few of the crabs will try to crawl out of the bucket to escape. While doing so, all of the other crabs will pull the escapee down to prevent it from escaping.

It's the mindset of "If I can't get out and live my life, then neither will you." Miserable people love company; it makes it more enjoyable for them.

So first, don't be a crab! Support those around you and be happy for their success, especially if they're your friends. Second, don't hang around crabs! When you hang around those types of people, they will do everything they can to prevent you from being confident, successful, and achieving your dreams.

Find friends that have big goals like you do and truly want what's best for you. Not only will your relationship be healthier and happier, but reaching your goals will be easier when you have a solid group of people on your side. So, if you don't already have a circle of friends who will help you achieve your goals, it's time to start finding them. If you already have an amazing friend group, then keep them around for as long as possible. Ask for support and do everything you can to support them in their endeavors.

If you have a group of crabby friends, guess what? It's time to cut them out of your life. I know that sounds harsh, but it's necessary. This is one of the hardest things to do, and honestly, most girls that read this book probably won't do it because they're too scared to hurt their friend's feelings. There's a good way to do this and a bad way to do this. It's important to be honest with them, but don't feel like you have to justify your reason for doing it. Remember that YOU are most important, not your friends' feelings. Your future is the main thing that you need to be concerned about, and if they're not supporting you and your future, then they need to go.

I know several kids from my high school that didn't understand the importance of the people in their life. I remember one kid in particular who was the star of the baseball team. He was a tremendous athlete with so much potential. He started getting calls from college coaches to play for their schools. His grades were decent, but he couldn't seem to get away from the wrong crowd. Of course, he had good friends and teammates around him, but these other kids were detrimental to his future. His junior year, he started getting into trouble, getting poor grades, and missing class. His other teammates were worried about the path he was going down, but he wasn't willing to cut the crabs out of his life. He never went on to play college ball, and I honestly haven't heard a thing about him since. Instead of putting himself first, he put the negative influences first, and it ruined any chance he had at achieving his goal of continuing his baseball career.

I guarantee that there are a million other stories like this of people who could have done big things but didn't hang out with the right people. So, remember this story next time you start surrounding yourself with the wrong crowd. This could be you too if you don't take control over your own life.

Dealing with Negative Parents and Coaches

Now, like I mentioned earlier, you don't have much control over your coaches, and you never have control over choosing your parents, so here's how to handle negative coaches or parents who are hurting your confidence...

Communication!

You must be willing to communicate how your coach or parents are affecting your confidence. If you don't ever tell them how you feel, they may never know that how they are treating you is hindering your growth, development, and love for your sport.

These conversations are never easy, but if you want to see a change, they must happen! Pull your parents or coaches aside and let them know that how they talk to you or how they treat you is making it hard for you to be confident. Tell them what you need from them instead.

Another thing you can do is have them read this chapter or let them know what you're learning about how the people in your life can make a big difference in your confidence.

I know this is easier said than done, but if they love you, which I know they do, they will listen. If you need some extra support, I'm here for you. All you have to do is email me at shay@alphagirlsoccer.com and I would love to help you through it.

Action steps to complete:

1. Identify the positive people in your life. Make a list of those people and thank them for their impact in your life.

2. Identify the negative people in your life and make a list.

3. Plan out the conversations you will have with those people to either cut them out or let them know you need more from them!

- nicole
- ella
- lily
- asby
- page
- chloe
- elizabeth
- mom
- dad
- KRIS!

- gavin
- gabi
- carleigh

Strategy #6: Pre-game Routines

"Until you're mentally ready you will never be physically prepared."

– Unknown

The last confidence building strategy that you're going to learn about is using pre-game routines. A pre-game or pre-performance routine is a set of actions that you do before every game. Pre-game routines can help you calm nerves, feel more confident, and get mentally prepared to play. Every time you complete your pre-game routine, your mind and body knows that it's time to play. Just like when you hear the bell go off before class and know it is time to walk to class, this routine is the signal that its go time!

The more prepared you are mentally, the more confident and ready you'll be when you step onto the field/court. I'm sure you've had a game where you were running late, you didn't sleep well or have a good meal, and were rushed to get to the field. I'm guessing you didn't feel well, weren't confident, and didn't play well that game.

An effective pre-game routine is one that will help you to feel calm yet ready, confident, and prepared to play both mentally and physically. A pre-game routine can be extremely simple, such as listening to the same song before each game. Alternatively, it can consist of several things that you do before your game.

Here's an example of what my pre-game routine looked like in college:

1. Eat a meal three hours before the game.
2. Visualize my success.
3. Get to the locker room 75 minutes before game time.
4. Get dressed and do my hair.
5. Eat small pre-game snack 60 minutes before game time
6. Dance my butt off for ten minutes with my teammates.
7. Settle in and listen to pre-game talk.
8. Get to the field.
9. Put my cleats on.
10. GO TIME!

Now, a youth player's pre-game routine may look much different as they likely don't have a locker room to dance with their awesome teammates, but the same principles can be applied. Your pre-game routine can be more complex like mine, or it can be simple, such as:

1. Eat a sandwich three hours before game.
2. Listen to your favorite music on the way to the game.
3. Visualize your success.
4. Get to the field and warmup.

The point is to do something that helps you forget about all the other stuff going in your life. Take the time to focus on one thing: THE GAME. It may take several attempts to nail down the pre-game routine that works best for you, but there's no right or wrong routine! Have fun with it. This should be something that you look forward to doing before every game. And if your current routine isn't working, don't be afraid to try something new until it sticks!

Action steps to complete:

1. Create your own pre-game routine—write it out!
2. Do your best to complete the routine before every game.
3. Adjust your routine as needed.

*do this Uhn season starts

Part 3
Success Tips

The Truth About Success

> *"Success isn't always about greatness. It's about consistency. Consistent hard work leads to success. Greatness will come."*
>
> – Dwayne 'The Rock' Johnson

In today's world, success seems like it happens overnight. You see your favorite athlete or celebrity on Instagram and see them as an overnight success. You wonder how they made it so fast while you're struggling to get on their level.

Well, let me tell you the secret to success…
there is no secret!

With social media being such a huge part of our lives, it is easy to look at other people and only see where they're at now. We often miss all of their hard work, sleepless nights, and failures along the way. Social media only shows the highlights of someone's life: the successes, lavish lifestyle, and celebrity status. However, if you were to actually have an honest conversation with those people, I guarantee that they'd tell you that it's been a process and took a lot of hard work to get where they are now.

Here's the other thing you must understand about success: the hard work you put in now won't show results until weeks, months, or years down the road. We live in a world of instant gratification, where we want to see results from our work TODAY. Very rarely will that happen. Here's the equation for success:

Small, smart choices + Consistency + Time = RADICAL RESULTS

Success compounds over time; if you take small actions toward your goals today, the results won't show up tomorrow or the next day. When you take consistent action every day, you will reach your goals, but it may not be for months or years down the road. That's why so many people never reach their goals or their true potential. They work so hard for a few weeks and don't see results. Then they give up. They don't understand that success is a process that takes time, consistency, and good habits.

Conversely, if you lose your focus and drive for a week, you may not see any major negative consequences right away. It will take time for those to show up. I learned this the hard way. At the beginning of this year, I started getting lazy and complacent. I stopped taking action on the small things to grow my business and help more players. I thought I could relax for a few months and that everything would continue to keep rolling. Fast forward to June, and it was one of the worst months I've ever had. Summer was supposed to be my busy time, yet I was struggling to fill up my programs and wasn't nearly as profitable I was the year before. I took a step back and reflected on what went wrong... bingo. My habits and actions earlier that year were the cause of my lack of results during the summer. I didn't fully understand this concept until it happened to me. Now, I make sure that I do small things every single day that will help me reach my goals, and I know that I will see results from the hard work I put in today.

So, learn from my mistakes and don't get discouraged when you don't see results right away. Don't give up on your hard work, because if you do, you will never see those results. However, if you keep working day after day, I promise that you will see results and that your hard work will pay off.

My Challenge for You: Get 1% Better Every Day

One of the most important things you can do for long lasting success, in sports or in life, is to strive to be better than you were the day before. The only person you should compare yourself to is you from yesterday! So, how can you be better than you were the day before? You don't need to be a whole new person and have crazy results to be better. All it takes is 1%. What can you do today to become 1% better than you were the day before?

I tell this to my players all the time who struggle with completing their soccer homework: **something is better than nothing**. If you don't have an extra two hours per week to practice your sport, that's okay, but can you find an extra ten minutes? My bet is that you can.

Getting 1% better every day can be as simple as you juggling at home for five more minutes, taking five extra free-throws at the end of practice, staying after class for five minutes to get help from your teacher, or pushing yourself harder at practice than you did yesterday.

I know 1% isn't a lot, but think about it, if you were to get 1% better each day, that's 365% better than you were last year! The change in the short term may seem insignificant, but when you take a look back at where you are now versus where you were last year, the growth will be huge.

When you take on this challenge and strive to be 1% better every day, there's no limit to how good and successful you can truly be in whatever you work towards; you just have to do the work.

Action steps to complete:

1. Get out your calendar and write down one thing you can do the next day to get 1% better. Repeat this every day.

2. Think about what you need to do to make this happen. Accountability from your parents or friends? Watching one less YouTube video to make time?

3. Every month, write out the awesome things you did last month that made you better this month.

- Visualization before move in
- schedule time

Creating Good Habits

> *Success is a few simple disciplines, practiced every day; while failure is simply a few errors in judgment, repeated every day.*
>
> –Jim Rohn

One of the most important things you need to establish if you want to be successful on and off the field is establishing good habits. Habits are the small decisions you make and actions you perform every day. According to researchers at Duke University, habits account for about 40 percent of our behaviors every day. This means that almost half of your behaviors are done out of habit without you even thinking about it!

Creating good habits is going to set yourself up to make good decisions that will ultimately help you succeed in whatever you do in life. Without habits, you have to rely on motivation and willpower to get things done. Motivation and willpower will run out when things get too tough, but habits stick.

The first thing you must know about creating good habits is that they take time to develop! If you want to create a habit of juggling for ten minutes every day, you must consistently practice every day until it no longer requires thought. What

I mean by this is that when you first start creating the habit, you will have to make a decision of whether or not you are going to go outside and juggle for ten minutes.

Every time you say "Yes!" and go for it, you move one step closer to creating a habit. Once you consistently put in the work, a habit will be formed. You will no longer have to decide whether to juggle or not. You'll just do it because it's a habit!

Here's your simple four step process to building a new habit:

1. Start with a small habit. Start with a habit that's so easy you don't need any motivation to do it. For example, instead of shooting 100 free-throws every day, start with just ten free-throws per day.

2. Increase your habit in small ways. If you shoot ten free-throws on the first day, shoot fifteen on the second day. Be 1% better than you were the day before, and the compound effect will really go to work

3. Don't miss more than two days in a row. If you miss a day, get back on track the next day. If you forget to shoot free-throws one day, that's okay! Just get back on track the next day so that you never miss more than two days in a row.

4. Be patient! Habits, just like success, take time to develop! Be patient and focus on the progress you've made so far.

Getting rid of bad habits is just as important as creating good ones! If you have a habit of scrolling through Instagram before you do your homework that will prevent you from getting your homework done before practice or cut into the time when you could be training on your own.

Here's your simple three step process for getting rid of bad habits:

1. Replace the bad habit with a good one. Instead of scrolling through Instagram, you could plan out your day for tomorrow.

2. Cut out the triggers that lead to that habit. If the first thing you do when you get home is have a soda and a cookie, then throw away the sodas and cookies (replace them with healthy snacks).

   For example, I have a bad habit of getting on Instagram when I'm working and I get bored or I'm switching between tasks. In order for me to get rid of that habit, I have to turn my phone on airplane mode and put it in my backpack so I'm not tempted to look at it.

3. Have an accountability partner. Find someone that will support you in getting rid of old habits. Ask them to hold you accountable when you mess up and celebrate with you when you stick to the plan.

Action steps to complete:

1. Write down three things that you want to improve on.
2. For each thing you want to improve on, write down one habit to focus on that will help you to reach your goal.
3. Take a look at your bad habits that deter you from reaching your goal and replace that habit with a healthy one.

- go on phone between tasks
  - airplane mode

- less napping / lazy time in middle of day
  - schedule rest time + work time

- biting nails when nervous
  - be more conscious

Goal Setting Mastery

> *"Setting goals is the first step in turning the invisible into the visible."*
>
> – Tony Robbins

If you want to achieve your biggest dreams, you must learn how to set goals. Goals are a huge part of your journey in getting what you really want out of life. Goals give you focus and direction in life. By setting goals, you give yourself a target to shoot for, motivation to accomplish tasks, and the power to avoid procrastination and distractions.

I can personally say that setting goals has been instrumental in my success as an athlete, coach, entrepreneur, and now author. Without setting goals, my focus would be all over the map, and I would be continually lost about what steps to take to be successful.

Heck, the power of setting goals is why you are reading this book right now! Without setting goals, I would have never finished this book and been able to help you on such a deep level. Back in April of 2019, I made a goal to write a book that same year. I didn't have a plan, but I stated that I wanted it to happen. Finally, in October, I sat down and got serious about my goal. I considered how many pages I was going to write per day, when the book would be finished, how many girls I wanted to help, etc.

Goal setting can seem very time intensive and take a lot of thought, but if you do it the right way, and take the steps necessary to achieve your goals, nothing can stop you, which is my goal for you. In this chapter, you're going to learn a simple, yet effective strategy for creating and achieving goals.

SMART Goals

I'm sure you've heard of the term "SMART goal," or some variation of that. Using the SMART goal method is a simple tool that you can use to plan and achieve your goals.

Here is my version of the SMART goal...

S- Specific

M- Measurable

A- Action oriented

R- Relevant/Realistic

T- Time bound

Let's dive a bit deeper into each of these components so it's crystal clear (just like your goals will be):

Specific: Clearly state exactly what you want to achieve. Your goal should be clear and specific.

Measurable: A measurable goal should state how much or how many. Put concrete numbers in your goals to know if you're on track.

Action-oriented: SMART goals are action-oriented, enabling you to create concrete steps that you will take to be successful. Identify what actions you need to take in order to reach that goal. A goal without action will never get accomplished.

Relevant/Realistic: This is about making sure that your goals matter to you. I like to think of this as your WHY. Why do you want to achieve this goal? What will this help you with in your life? Also make sure that the goal is realistic in nature.

Timely: Every smart goal needs a target date to reach that goal by. By having a deadline, you will stay motivated to accomplishing that goal by your target date.

Refer to the table below to get a better understanding of how to break down a SMART goal to create your own.

GOALS

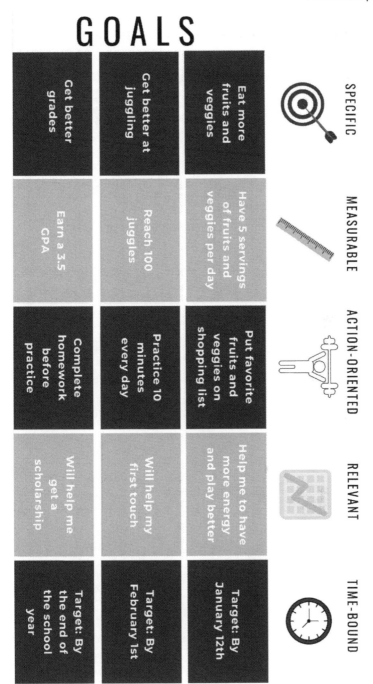

	SPECIFIC	MEASURABLE	ACTION-ORIENTED	RELEVANT	TIME-BOUND
	Eat more fruits and veggies	Have 5 servings of fruits and veggies per day	Put favorite fruits and veggies on shopping list	Help me to have more energy and play better	Target: By January 12th
	Get better at juggling	Reach 100 juggles	Practice 10 minutes every day	Will help my first touch	Target: By February 1st
	Get better grades	Earn a 3.5 GPA	Complete homework before practice	Will help me get a scholarship	Target: By the end of the school year

So instead of just saying, "My goal is to be a better soccer player," you can go deeper by using the SMART method. Here's what that goal would turn into: "I want to reach 100 juggles by February 1st in order to help me improve my first touch. I will do this by practicing for ten minutes every day."

For me, I set small weekly goals that help me achieve my biggest dreams. I would suggest setting new goals at least every month or every quarter (four times per year).

For example, here's when you can set new/review last quarter's goals:

Quarter 1 January: Set goals for January-March

Quarter 2 April: Review last quarter goals. Set new goals for April-June

Quarter 3 July: Review last quarter goals. Set new goals for July-September

Quarter 4 October: Review last quarter goals. Set new goals for October-December

How to Achieve Your Goals

Now that you know how to set a SMART goal, it's time to do the real work to take the steps necessary to achieve that goal. Most people never actually do this step, which is why most people never accomplish their biggest goals and dreams.

Anyone can set a goal, but it takes good habits and discipline to achieve those goals.

Here's how to achieve your goals:

1. Put them somewhere visible: Once you have written down your goals, place them somewhere where you will see them every day! If you write your goals and stuff them in your backpack, you'll forget about them within the next 24 hours. Place them on your fridge, mirror, nightstand, or as the background on your phone. The more you see it, the more likely you are to take action on them.

2. Share your goals: Share your goals with someone that you deeply do not want to disappoint. This could be a parent, friend, teammate, or mentor. Sharing your goals will serve as two purposes. First, it makes your goals come to life and seem more real. The universe works in crazy ways when you state what you want in life and take action to make it happen. Second, by sharing your goals, you will have someone to hold you accountable to getting it done. It's easy to give up on a goal when no one knows about it. It's much harder to give up when you know someone is counting on you.

3. Create an action plan: I like to call this, reverse engineering your goals. Here is the simple 3-step process to reverse engineer your goals to see consistent results. Write down your answer to these questions for each goal you set:

- What can I do today to get closer to my goals?

- What steps do I need to take in next seven days to achieve my goal?

- What steps do I need to take in the next 30 days to achieve my goal?

    Make sure you do this for every goal you set! By breaking down your action steps, it will help you stay disciplined, on track, and moving towards your goal.

4. Track your progress: Tracking progress will help you to stay disciplined by looking at your small wins along the way. By tracking your progress, it will give you insight into if you're on the right path or if you need to make changes. Many times, when working on accomplishing a goal, you'll find that you're way off track or that something you're doing isn't working. That's why it's important to track, so that you can readjust and change what you're doing if needed.

Action steps to complete:

1. Set one SMART goal for each of the following areas of your life: school, sport, and health.

2. Reverse engineer each goal and write specific actions you can take today, seven days, and thirty days.

3. Place your goals somewhere where you'll see them every day

4. Find an accountability partner and share your goals with them

---

School; review consistently so I don't have to cram

- review for placement exam
- plan a weekly study routine
- execute routine when classes start

Sport: improve blocking

- review foot work nightly
- visualization + full effort on reps
- weight room reps

health; stay on track in dining hall

- X
- look at menu before going
- make a routine

73

Leadership

> *"If you're not a leader on the bench, don't call yourself a leader on the field. You're either a leader everywhere or nowhere."*
>
> – Abby Wambach

In my opinion, leadership is one of the most important skills you will learn while playing your sport. It will translate to every area of your life going forward. Developing leadership skills now will help you become a better teammate, player, student, friend, and family member for the rest of your life. When you're done playing your sport, leadership will play a huge role in your success in the professional world as well. Whether you work in a small team, huge company, or even by yourself, you will use leadership skills at one point or another to accomplish goals and get things done!

In fact, according to research conducted by Ernst & Young, 94% of women who hold C-suite level positions (CEO, CFO, COO, etc.) are former athletes. Of those, 52% played sports at the collegiate level. This speaks to the importance of why playing sports and developing leadership skills now is so important!

There are a lot of misconceptions about what it takes to be a good leader and what kind of person you have to be in order to be respected and effective in that role. Being a leader is not about having power; it's about leading a group of people to achieve a common goal. A leader is someone who wants the best for the team as a whole. You lead by influencing people through the way you behave and carry yourself.

Anyone can be a leader. You don't have to be the loudest or most outgoing person to be a great leader. It certainly can help to be outgoing because communication is a big part of leadership, but some of the best leaders are introverts. Introverts have the ability to more effectively connect with people one-on-one or in intimate settings.

For me, I was never the loudest or most outgoing. I hated, and still hate, any form of confrontation. Having to call out a teammate or address issues among the team made me squirm. However, as team captain I was a committed hard worker and passionate about the goals we were trying to achieve. I used my strengths to be the best leader I could be. It's important to know your strengths as a leader and use those strengths to lead the team.

Below are ten qualities of a good leader. After reading them, go through and highlight or write down your top five strongest qualities.

1. Great Communication

Not only do you need to communicate to deliver information, but you need to use communication to share ideas and your vision for the team. It's important to know how to communicate with each member of your team. Everyone has different communication styles, so it's your job as the leader to know your own communication style and that of the team. One of your teammates may be okay with taking criticism while another may have a harder time. In that case, as a good leader, it's important to communicate with them differently in order to help them and the team.

In addition to being able to get your message across, being an effective communicator often means closing your mouth and opening your ears to listen. The best leaders are ones that can listen intently in order to solve problems.

2. Commitment / Passion

No one wants to follow a leader that isn't oozing with passion. As a leader, you need to be passionate and committed to the team's goals. Being passionate doesn't mean that you need to be boisterous or come off as "extra." Your passion for the team will come to life in the hard work you put in on the field. The more passionate and committed you are, the more that will reflect in the actions of your team.

3. Humility

When it comes to being a leader, it can be easy to become obsessed with your status. Nothing is more of a turn-off than a leader who thinks they're better than everyone else. Being humble and vulnerable with the team will make you more relatable and effective in building trust with the team.

4. Work Ethic

One of the best ways to become a great leader is to lead by example. The harder you work, the more respect you'll earn from your team. As a result, they will also work harder to reach your team's goals. Good leaders aren't afraid to roll up their sleeves and do the dirty work.

5. Positivity

One of the most important qualities of a great leader is the sense of positivity that spreads to everyone around them. As a leader, there will be many moments of frustration and disappointment, but it's important to take a positive approach in handling these situations. Make positivity a habit and your teammates will follow.

6. Empathy

Empathy is the ability to understand and share the feelings of another person from their point of view. As a leader, possessing this trait allows you to connect with your teammates on a deeper level. When you show empathy, you build their trust and become someone that they admire and respect. It has also been said that women quite often make better leaders than men because of our ability to be openly empathetic and vulnerable, so use that to your advantage!

7. Integrity / Honesty

Without honesty and integrity, no real success is possible. In order for you to become a good leader (and person in general), you must show integrity in all you do, both on and off the field. This builds trust and a culture of honesty throughout the entire team. Without trust, the team will fall apart sooner than later.

8. Confidence

If you are not confident about your own abilities or the abilities of the team, your team will never follow you. Practice good body language by standing tall, making eye contact, and controlling your fidgeting. The more confident you are, the more confident your team will be in your ability to lead. Your confidence will radiate to your team members and make the team as a whole much more confident in achieving your goals.

9. Inspirational

As a leader, one of your biggest responsibilities will be to inspire others and get them to see your vision and the vision of the team. By inspiring others to be all in, the team will run like a well-oiled machine because everyone is on the same page in doing what it takes to achieve the team goals.

10. Open Minded

A good leader needs to be open to new ideas and open to change. There will be times as a leader where you make mistakes or head down the wrong path. Open mindedness is all about responding to feedback and taking action to correct course. Never be too good to learn and grow.

It is okay if you found it hard to narrow your strengths down to just five of the traits above or struggled to find five things that you excel at! The point is to be aware of what your strengths are as a leader. Leadership isn't some one size fits all solution. Each and every person will have a different leadership style and ways of effectively leading a team.

By being aware of your strengths, you can use those strengths to your advantage to adopt your own unique leadership style. On the other hand, it's important to be aware of the characteristics that you may need to improve upon. Although your ability to inspire others may not be at the top of your list now, you must be aware of that and practice in order to improve in that area. Every single person will possess different strengths and weaknesses. The key to being a great leader is to lead with your strengths and continue to improve upon other areas.

Just like learning how to shoot a basketball can be practiced and improved, so can these leadership skills. Like you've read about throughout this whole book, it takes awareness, a growth mindset, and consistent effort to get better at anything.

Action steps to complete:

1. Identify your top five leadership quality strengths from the list above.

2. Rank those five leadership quality strengths from 1-10 (1 being strongest and 10 being weakest).

3. Take action to lead with your strengths and improve upon your weaknesses.

- work ethic 10
- communication 7
- passion 9
- Open minded 8

- positive 6

Closing

Congrats on finishing the book! You've completed the first step in improving your mindset, growing your confidence, and changing your life. Of course, your work is far from over. In order for you to truly change and grow your confidence, you must complete the action steps at the end of each chapter. Not only once, not only twice, but on a daily basis. At first it will seem daunting and time-consuming, but once you create a habit of changing your inner voice, visualizing, having good body language, and using affirmations, it'll become natural. Remember, just like any skill you are trying to learn, changing your mindset and building your confidence takes time, energy, and consistent practice.

If you haven't completed each action item yet, go back and do it now. It doesn't have to be perfect or even close to it. Remember, progress over perfection. Something is better than nothing.

If you're feeling hesitant or doubt whether you'll be able to follow through on practicing these habits on a daily basis, that okay! It's normal to feel this way. Changing your habits and doing something new never feels natural. You may feel awkward and unnatural when you first practice visualization, work on your weaknesses, and begin building new habits, but they key is to do it anyway.

Consider the rewards. When you commit to the process of changing your mindset and improving your confidence, you will be building the foundation for success in every area of your life for the rest of your life. Your mindset is your most powerful tool to get what you want out of life, and you have total control over it.

When you have a growth mindset and confidence in your abilities, no one or nothing can stop you. Sure, you'll fail a lot along the way, have people tell you that you can't do it, and feel like giving up. That's all part of the process. They key is to use the tools and skills that you've developed from this book to fight past those obstacles and to be strong enough to NEVER give up on your dreams, and most importantly, to never give up on yourself. You are your most important asset. You have the ability to live your live the way you want, on your terms. So go out there and live it!

I'm here for you, and I believe in you. Now it's time for YOU to believe in YOU! You got this!

A Special Invitation

Now that you're done reading the entire book and the action steps in each chapter, I want to help you!

Here are the steps for you and your parents to complete:

Step 1: Visit my website at www.alphagirlconfidence.com to learn how I can personally help you in achieving lifelong confidence.

Step 2: From there you can book a free strategy session, we will go deeper into how I can help and go over full game plan to help you improve your confidence on and off the field.

Step 3 (for parents): Join us inside our free Facebook group for parents and coaches. In this group I host live trainings for parents every week that will help you to better support your daughter in becoming more confident on and off the playing field.

Request to join here:
www.facebook.com/groups/alphagirlconfidence

About the Author

Shay Haddow is an expert coach and speaker on confidence and mindset for female athletes. Having worked with hundreds of youth female athletes and college teams from across the country, she's empowered girls from all walks of life to strengthen self-belief to play and live confidently.

As the founder of Alpha Girl Confidence, host of the Alpha Girl Confidence Podcast, and Author of the best-selling book "She the Confident," Shay is widely regarded for her insights on confidence and mindset by parents, coaches, and players around the country.

After overcoming her own struggles of self-doubt and lack of confidence, she knew that it was her life's calling to provide female athletes with the coaching that she wished she had. Shay is dedicating her life to empowering female athletes to uncover their greatest superpower of all, allowing them to break free from their limitations and achieve their biggest dreams. She does this through her signature coaching program, her podcast *The Alpha Girl Confidence Podcast*, and this book.

To contact Shay about coaching and speaking opportunities, or to subscribe to her podcast, visit:

www.alphagirlconfidence.com

Connect with Shay on Twitter & Instagram by following
@shayhaddow

Join the free Facebook page for parents and coaches at
www.facebook.com/groups/alphagirlconfidence

scrimmage day reflection:
you did a good job in the start,
you were nervous + missed the
first serve, + then let her
comment affect you. your serve
recieve was average, but for you
it was not good enough because you usually excel at serve
recieve + stay very calm. she
pulled you too early + you also
let that affect you, the main
issue is that you didn't push
yourself to recover from the
mental block + let her words
affect how you used the other
opportunities
that she
gave you. you lost focus
+ started doubting which results
in being slower... she
likes you be you are
fast, confident, energetic, + loud.
dont let yourself loose the good
qualities that she sees in you.
you also need to learn from